my maiden cowboy names

Winner of the
2008 T. S. Eliot Prize

The T. S. Eliot Prize for Poetry is an annual award sponsored by Truman State University Press for the best unpublished book-length collection of poetry in English, in honor of native Missourian T. S. Eliot's considerable intellectual and artistic legacy.

Judge for 2008: Grace Schulman

my maiden cowboy names

victoria brockmeier

Truman State University Press
New Odyssey Series

Published by Truman State University Press, Kirksville, Missouri USA
tsup.truman.edu
© 2008 Victoria Brockmeier
New Odyssey Series
All rights reserved

Cover image: *Credences 3* (©) Jess Collins Trust and used by permission. From the collection of Robert and Anne Bertholf.

Cover design: Teresa Wheeler
Type: Minion Pro © Adobe Systems Incorporated; ITC Tiepolo © Adobe Systems Incorporated, and a registered trademark of International Typeface Corporation.
Printed by: Thomson-Shore, Dexter, Michigan USA

Library of Congress Cataloging-in-Publication Data

Brockmeier, Victoria, 1978–
  My maiden cowboy names / Victoria Brockmeier.
    p. cm. — (New odyssey series)
  ISBN 978-1-931112-81-9 (alk. paper) — ISBN 978-1-931112-82-6 (pbk. : alk. paper)
  I. Title
  PS3602.R632M9 2008
  811'6—dc22

                                                                    2008027219

The paper in this publication meets or exceeds the minimum requirements of the American National Standard for Information Sciences—Permanence of Paper for Printed Library Materials, ANSI Z39.48–1992.

contents

acknowledgments

Grateful acknowledgment is made to the editors of the following journals in which poems in this collection have previously appeared.

Spoon River Poetry Review: "?" and "work of laura"
Pleiades: a journal of new writing: "medea"
Chelsea: "cow tipping," "on a boy named for war, enrolled in my afternoon comp class," "the space from polestar to dogstar," and "pastoral w/dirt under its fingernails"
Inkwell: "lark: to thieve as though in open country," "high school sweetheart," "a gravid eve" (as "days gravid"), and "singer of tales"
Natural Bridge: "red*star"
Arkansas Review: "thirteen ways of looking at kudzu"
LIT: "from the wagon" and "honk for support"
New Letters: "an emancipation"

,

sing in me, muse, of the bits left out—
notched corners & cobwebs swept from them,

a hexerie, a woman of words, bodeful winds
that sleet savage into midwinter; sing of the woodbine

weeding its way through her garden,
her rough-cut porch's wood, the ridges, whorls, its slant

of tin roof, sing mountains black as green,
red as black, a slow shrug of the plains, eaten

to karst & like to crumble underfoot; call
through the thin curve, the gravel

rank with grasses, vervain, squaw weed, oak leaves
piled autumn on autumn in the ditches

& slime molds creeping in the charnel cool. fill me with
every snipped-out *o* & open my throat

with the earthed-over aria of blood washed to blush
dwindling through gravel & into a creek, of bones

scattered, roots between, bearing witness
to the land's befretted breach:

ninefold lady of harp, mix these round bodies
in mine & in the alchemy of light let in

pour them forth: canting chorus, frayed;
multitudinous tongues, startled throats.

1

"before the dogtooth violets
(which were yellow or white & not violet at all)
pushed up their spotted leaves"

house that burned itself down

it dreams in heat. it dreams in orange flame.
quarried; bared. limestone mines gnaw out
the ground on three sides: behind, a cemetery thrusts

into the air. a century stirs in the ground, more, bones
shifting from their bodies' original lay, webbed moulder
breathing itself down, & smaller. for an instant the house

looks whole, square, lit from within
as if by electric light. but its paint has shredded
from wood aged gray; its roof
sags, broken to mule-back by fire then weather.

how much longer can it stand, deedless. how many
long droughts, how much ice splitting its joins. tornados

twisting by a mile off, or less. shreds of weak light
knocking around inside, shaking at its beams & bursting
rotted floorboards from below. the highway growling
into its cellar, the cellar wrestling that growl

around & back. when there's rain
it blackens the boards all over again, raises slime
& fattens splinters. holes for windows

gape, blank as if shutting out winter; snatches
of sky, headlights shoot back dully
from what chinked glass remains.
they want something more to cut into pieces.

merciful, meager, struck through the veins

i. honk for support

it's my sign, more than taurus ever was
& i carry it like a calf. weather is the kind of friend
who borrows your car to rob convenience stores:
he's got his august arms around me this week, rasping
angry creases where he pulls seams taut over my skin. management
is the enemy. apathy is the enemy. silence
is the enemy. unfair to workers is the enemy.

they're my lines, more than they ever were
the local's. new pavement glares up, furiously static,
half heat, half noise, a blast unconfined to its moment. all
the footsteps here are mine, the migraine
& greenish haze, johnny-on-my-picket-walk.
sunstroke is the enemy. half a day's pay to pace
like tomorrow's coming in on waxed wings.

batter, june bug, our season's remnant, crash
& keep buzzing. even upside down. i have seen better days
only in the lines on my palm. workers of the world
don't impede my view, clouds don't blunt
these shadows. still, i can't see an end to this strike.

scabs on my legs where i scratched out bites, burns
—even they have crossed the line.

ii. from the wagon

when the carnival left me in kansas city—
was slim-wristed, slim of thighs, hair a territorial red
that darkened from my life in the shade. resolute:
got my card for the local #216, got my downtown.
my central air, my modern, my collared shirts
& shoes that tied. cattle here are an axiom
of the landscape; so with hills that round like breasts,

bellies, fat with the fare of our location. meat, here;
salt, here. axioms of the table. we root ourselves,
cannibals, rabbits alternately, auspiced to a single stretched nerve:
gone to ground. slightest, sharpest darling, aboriginal
to shindug sawdust, to torchlight, tossed change. now
i am settled—which is to say, full of regret. bars
indent my forehead above the back way's metallic stink, nights

& murky days, & sleeping through ice. municipal. our ratcatchers, our
three-legs: lived more like the living. our trained mules
wheezed but from dust & pollen, not the permanent
stinging smoke through which the skyline
wills out the stars. this is the end of grace
here where the carnival moved on, end of light-as-air.

my skin paled to show freckles & i resigned myself
to muffled time. went to ground on the eleventh floor.

iii. canticle for fiddle & drum

an earlier body, my brisés, my castanets' clatter
would have arrested passers-by as this cramped dispute
bleached near to vanishing on its ground
can't hope. i miss the firelight, the shiver
of piccolo like birch tea. gritty boards
beneath bare feet, & shuffle, & spin, leap,
flare of scarf hem flung away over my knees: then dirt

kissed away in warm dark. the seasons ardent,
jigging in their breezes, moving wherever birds would, scrubland
to lowland to various coasts, pondside, hillside,
under a fattened moon, under a tin sheet propped up
under a ragged sky emptying itself of thunder & water,
the gentle cries, the hush then ebb. barebacked balance,
arms a valley: dance touched in points to the rhythm

of early blood. after all we are bodies first & bound
to words only once taught to speak. carillons rang
across my skin with the waves lapping over lily leaves,
pine paneling creaked & sighed, sheets crumpled
to cover cast-off skirts. what rare fortune to have laughed

nights away in radiant vertigo, when meteors
shot home, when spangles, coins—fell into place.

iv. loving vulcan

forearms blackened by grease & with shoulders
good to pull a train from its tracks:
he lifted & slew me fine. through the early dark
of a few february nights i mapped him, us both hungry
to embrace domain, salt-skinned, friable. the cold sun
pinked my cheeks, blissed beneath smudges
from his steelhandler's hands. he said *pretty*

like it was my name, breath a cannonade
over the moth's-wing-shaped shadows on my back—
& how i'd flex to his touch, my body one slow
mesmerized smile. light & movable as a reflection
on a cold river, trilled out as pound & sway
beat a field for may morris. love was easy;
i'd never yet fought morning over its indifference.

tambourine-bright, the ring fit cool as melting sugar, cool
as whistling with a vinca leaf—people drink champagne
for this feeling, the archer-boy's luscious poison, sparkly,
tarry, tipping the buds of every tree we kissed under,
sealing those winter nubs for one explosive quake

of green across brown. i could feel the red in my blood
singing hymeneals, canny, clear to the ends of my fingers.

v. a gravid eve

st joe's hospital was an easter lily's open gut, starkly
stretched in greens, in white, to clam our palms. halls
echoed like empty houses, the healthy & sick quiet
as pages turning over each other. trees outside, scarved
with scarlet by fall's first sure frost. big-bellied
me, two floors below my pink-&-ultrasound ground:
trauma ward. my hand in my little son's, his skin

a salamander's, our stares puddled on the carpet
we were so quiet only the ghosts heard us speaking—
& there were ghosts. our old one-armed strongman,
soap sellers, itinerant bookbinders, transom men, roving
this city by its shadows, traceable in want
of their boatman. son & i wound stories in twine
of more living hues, spun them, spun again til a girl nurse

(i saw her wiry body twisted around a trapeze, painted
bright with cheers) wheeled out my husband. the line took
his days, then his nights, then the arm he'd used to hold up
the damaged sky—weeks later the fever woke us, bruising
beneath our eyes & gravelly voices. one year, we'd have.

that brown river rolled east & we did not. "silver footed,"
he said, "dance & all shall be made well."

vi. singer of tales

sheherazade had nothing on me. countless & one nights
on a carpet of charmed plywood, wedged into the rattly top
of a rail trestle. gray autumn below where the dead
never walk, wary of the roads' relentless thrum,
how pallid a place, how narrow-lipped, & we clung
lean, pared, with orchids' tenacious fix over bark. down & up,
tottery in storms: crowdless ropewalkers. each night

i leaned out to read from the constellation code—
the fox who smiled twice, perseus, how baba yaga
lost her house, the legend of why things fall. fortune
cards spread. postcards. grandmother's ovid sewn
in floppy cowhide. husband, laid deep; son
fated to plunge from a ruddier sky
& land badly; bitten, trim daughter early & proud

to master every cross. when her first tooth wobbled
like an apple & fell i promised it would grow a dragon.
we were yet too brute to dine on air, bellies caving
& then our legs, wind chipping our cheeks; two snows
before we curled into walls & a door. long ago we closed

the soft spots in our skulls & so learned to lie:
so high, we were still shut dumb of heaven's everyday.

vii. an emancipation

that girl, daughter, a clench, gifted
as an owl. stars pricked the sky through, the day
she was born, bright & whirling as pixies' knives.
she & her brother were barren children
of drought years: nickel-smooth, ringing together. he rode
out one summer to hunt the aurora, the way ice
gnashes at pine needles, to beard a mountain

above its kilt of cloud; after, the girl took law
to her bed & sees me mostly in the sweltry dreams
we share. harbinger, she is, auburn atropos.
her grandmother lived the unsheathed call
of peregrine, her gypsy skin, her irish blood
& love, her voudou. kissing her left my lips
with the tang of tea leaves, the gift of flight; vines

wreathed her hands, brick into brown, haunted—
so, she marked her resistance to the malady
of traveling only by road. she bequeathed me india
with its trunk up & other charms that found no home
in the pockets i offered or in my vernacular grasp.

accidental photograph: my daughter's sclerotic hands,
constitutional. the avian in her has migrated for good.

unseaming season

Alewel's Country Meats, Warrensburg, MO

the fifth grade field trip was never to a field
but to what came after for chawing, snorting,
shuffling creatures ruminating the length of the bus route;

we'd seen them whole & in pieces but never the states
between. shaggy charolais & herefords, glossy angus,
hump-necked brangus: white, red, & black, colors

more basic than the primaries. but here who could tell
what hides had wrapped over what'd been now
cut down, packeted in crisp paper. *steer,*

we heard, from a word that meant *broad,* or *husky*
like my little brother's clothes. square you could draw,
shoulder-hip-hip-shoulder, bred for more years

than a month in history class to carry
bigger steaks per pound of bone, to fit together
in the feed lot. but so boxy they needed help

birthing little ones: long rubber gloves, old towel
—some of us had. bred. gobbeted. we took the line
backward, cashier first, then packing, then carving

where a boy whose dad had sheriffed the county
long as any of us could read election signs split
fat from meat like parting curtains. bottle-bottom glasses,

thatch of hair, slouching into point-toed boots,
still frankenstein-tall. but here the doctor,
parceling out his corpse: white to rendering,

red to packing. herded once more contrariwise & we saw the beast
whole, miraculously calm. sharp buzz, smoke,
then what you expect before the monster rises: the eyes

open then back & closed. but still. a hot wire cut clean
through its neck, like in shop class cutting boomerangs
from styrofoam. who could help but think *barbecue!*

the warm wet air & the cook smell. the red washing
toward a drain, swirling nearly clear on its way.
like hosing off a patio, like doing dishes. the carver boy

hollered our class around back in his scratchy-record voice:
lunchtime, with halved kc strips. a little blood
clears us of this hunger. & tender. good marble in that cut.

lark: to thieve as though in open country

soft, tapered fingers & knuckles, barely
dimpled: her hands could belong
to any eleven-year-old. not her mouth,

thin lips, quick flash of crowded teeth, showing dark fillings
when she laughs; she watches bones ripple
her skin from beneath as she picks over

mounded pints of blackberries, inky
with sun hidden inside. swollen, shining fruit;
meadow scent; warm in midmorning. to buy

something so perishable. to lose an afternoon
in the tang of new-from-the-cane, electric

& smart in her mouth. the breakable black.
to savor a few but have mold rise between the rest
like slow fog from the river to its banks.

she'd crossed its headwaters once on tiptoe,
dark, northern water that had swirled rock into knots

& that tasted of clover when she took a palmful
to her tongue. too-young fingers flick one berry,
another, up her cuff. only what can be carried

without bruising. what makes for half an hour
perched above that brown beast of a river. chatter, chatter,

heat lightning, horse show, spur off the interstate,
frogging season, so they'll watch her face & not her hands. skins

tauten, then slip back from each pocket of pulp & juice,
bloody as red in her mouth & green, pungent,
even the blackest berries. they've waited

as long as they could, stripped from their tangled
canes & at the far edge of ripe: to have their tart

boiled thick, sugared down, slurred into quart jars?
what comes unsealed. what can't be packed away.

flyover

Follow us

—motto of the USAF 509th bomb wing

clumsy, busty july afternoon: two shortalled girls
shampoo a boy's hair with dirt while he laughs & slaps
the ground. the caption will read, "budding cosmetologists

take their first customer." it will read, "daughter
of tsgt. jacob anders, daughter of lt. anne mchenry,
son of sgt. felix vasquez," immortalized in halftone
for the base's cheery spirits. but a steady growl

through the earth, or the air, & one glossy wing
arrows through the haze of just-harrowed pasture, looping
cursive against clouds & the cocksure blue

overhead. a teacher in a corduroy skirt tilts up
the few chubby, lagging chins so no one will miss—
what? how to describe the simple, inky black,
the cartoon edge, knowing what load it bore?

"stealth shows off for its youngest fans."
a few years back, up the highway:
a thousand-some kids dragged jacketless

from second period to shiver as november scoured
our cheeks. clouds above heavy,
seamless as pewter, the air forcing ice

into our lungs' lowest lobes: a slack, unified "ooh"
at the flat wedge roaring toward us, its launch
straight up. "local students," the caption read,

"observe." as a state holiday, as a mandate, as custom
or an execution. as an experiment. unimpressably teenaged,
we headed in without a cue; we had notes
to pass. stiff fingers to clench & unclench.

sun shoots back from wide, dark eyes; shines
on new buttons & newer teeth. a teacher's hand
tames a breeze from baby-afro frizz. angular scrap
of something larger, black notch cut out of the day.

cow tipping

you'd never think they'd tumble
the way they do, docile as a vase of sunflowers
knocked off a table. or how heavy

the sound is, how complex—you feel it
in your ribs as shoulder hits the earth

before haunch. how long they take
getting up. how their eyes give back
the whole moon, the shabby clouds

tearing themselves up to stretch toward dawn,
& they have to heave themselves up,

give it a couple goes. the grasses pulse
with crickets, katydids, fingernail-sized frogs,
all that *come on, come on*, swimming in mist,

then upwards, & you'd never know. unless you resist
the adrenaline & step back only a few feet

after pushing, hard, at that angus bulk—
you'll never feel your hands tingle, palms
printed with bristly hair, never notice how the hide

is cold with dew at first but instantly
warm beneath, instantly mammal,

never get the shock in your wrists
from toppling a near half-ton of muscle
wrapped over bone. you have to hold yourself

in air that slips across your skin
like charmeuse, let your shoes

sink into the turf a little as the head
swings around, drunk with broken sleep
like any animal, puffing out rank milk breath.

when it finally gains its hooves,
it could charge, pulp your suddenly fleshy frame,

that weight could shatter your clavicle like a branch
split away from a log & chewed to gimcrack
by termites. you'd never see, though,

unless you hung around, how after it rises
it only shuffles its hocks through the pasture,
the mist, the whirring bugs, to surround itself
with the shine & heave & steam of other broad backs.

high school sweetheart

seven months of hard hands & immaculate sheets,
my pleas folded into pearly baths, a stolen
garter belt, skin glitter; to no end. i craved the sound

of my pulse at spate in my own ears, in my knuckles, wanted to curl
around his feet & ankles like floodwater, to invade him,
to persist like the scent of amber resin, fall-harvest honey

warm from morning on its stony pot. came an afternoon
i met him at my door, stark pink & jittery, smiling—
mostly i remember his stare dull as marbles

dug from the garden. six years after, given up
& split from him, a low brown
still shades my spine, gauntening the bones' shape

unless you press the skin to the side & see, this is a scar.
which i explain as, he had some problem with beds.
couches too. i could have been thrown on a wheel

& never known different. two years he had me
with roses i watched hang from my bedroom vent, turning
& withering to their permanent season. i whispered, yesterday,

tomorrow, like a long autumn where the wind
rattled leaves over pavement & windowpanes,
where corn stalks clacked together at night, gibbering & dumb.

work of laura

i am eating only the slenderest flowers:
sympathetic magic. nasturtiums are the hottest, & soon
i will burn my way out. will be blue & black
& white only, angles inked on a page. the high hollow

between my breasts where my ribs divide away, spartan line
of shoulder to wrist studded midway by elbow, point
of hip, shadowed temple: my devotions, this is clarity,

a climb. last week i hit 100 but am back down. my bones
are of iron, oiled gray, weighting me to this crust, turf
where cattle shuffle their muddy hocks. it would help

if i were finely drawn, like shadbush twigs, like wire,
drawn as to the high & sharp, as a carriage,

as the curtains between the planked seat
inside & god's murmuring body. i don't want
to write about blood but it is thick
& inevitable. began today to wean my veins
to light & breath. i'll be beautiful

when i am gone. i'll exhale light
like the moon breathing out her reflection, blow
this corpse free of the filament beneath,
ash, shrapnel, granulate, ad astra. when i am thin

as silk i will float & ripple, you'll see—
stars peeping through my skin, stretched & scraped
to vellum. i'll fold myself to wallet size
& slip between your pages.

"she jumped right down to the paddle wheel
& rode its fins toward the water"

pastoral w/dirt under its fingernails

we have the roughest trees, the most brutal green
around. we raise suspicion in fields
& when it drains the soil we rotate it out
for soybeans or alfalfa. it's hard land

to farm, angry land, indian land, bedeviled
by ghosts who stir mists fancy-dancing & lay dead brown hands
on the occasional agued forehead; they're why tilled
acres here burn so fierce, why rain marauds

so restlessly through the summer months. memory
swims, fish in our ponds, pale green, silver,
red, dodges in & out of the shadows,
their brownish green—the history

of never forgetting our place. always had
a soft spot for minnows & other creatures
bred for bait, worms that abandon the earth
when storms glut the mosses & soften roots, worms

that do their grandaddies' drought dances
in the dirt roads & marigold beds, plead
on asphalt in curvy text. boot heels sound
& leave behind two marks

to punctuate. farmers, hands inked
with fertilizer, black loam, a surfeit
of seed & row, with gear grease—refuse
the sudden straightening. the way pasture

shrinks a trace, craftless, suffocated
& stiff, unetched by annelid wakes. hard land,
stubborn land. spring is skittish here, the sky
fighting with the wind & the uncertain sun. it's a world

of waiting for the trumpet vine & kudzu to reconquer
our roads. i want this poem to leave the taste
of the mud-salad ozarks in your mouth.
i want you to feel the mission in our voiceless soil.

they are mountains they are hills

two hundred miles a hearthstone
crumpling america's undertraveled midparts to curves
of fallen broadcloth to deep hillsides
just high enough to look soft blaze of green tracked
by roads drawn across as if by a razor

by wagoneers who dropped out of the gold rush halfway
their childer grew to stake down unarable acres
bread-fed faces those blocky
shoulders & barrel bodies shaped to plant
but quick between storms

by the plains & what produce got trucked into them bagged greasy
from wax mealy what should be firm
crisp what should give—peaches came in
dry & tough as february to our gall bounds

the dry summer grasses the sumac
how one week in july would brittle
the state shroud every leaf in dun weeds
rustling like paper
where heat meant burn not boil

i've learned humility before bayou & the subtropical
one season this easy winter like no time at all
so time lost so skinks & carpenter ants savaged

here on the delta it's every breath
thick tasting like mud flat sky
midnight a close orange glow the lake stitched
with burnoff at night & by day plantation architecture

beloved bad memories scrim swamp from air
stars lost in the drone
of piston axle scorch polish & drawl

every breath the tin sound of walls
barring moths rain & moths wings abeat
each dodge into a new iteration of ache

talk here flutters like flags
sunny rows flapping in a scrap breeze
that hunts its own tail

i want brambles wrapped back around me
dumb & wild lash me as i pass
let me bend to those lying blooms the redbud
which is purple the jimsonweed with its friendly
silver trombones the touch-me-not spurred yellow orange
weal found shy at the woods' edge

ragweed's rank favors sunflower warmed walnut & oak & sycamore
pollens loosed do-see-doing through the air late
in the hot part of every year with the leather musk
of leaves whispering brown & whole

from harvest almost to harvest again a scent that fastens onto roads
threatens to disappear you in cocooning bindweed mess of honeysuckle
slow but the tangle drops still like a tarp

after dusk those hollows
cool so slow where grannies' spit
mixes with runoff nitrous bitter
with the rusted sweat of the mountains
springs that trickle up from caves & leach dark
these ponds are oracles severe & sharp-tasting

let me kneel to your fallow fields burnt black
thunderheads that pile up like clay dug
to put in a mine a bridge a root cellar a storm cellar

let me bend down & drink
even the silt even the yellow
beer-breathed sun slanting through
even the muck of uncaught fish

i want sand & gravel scuffing down
my shins into the tops of my feet
pressed into the muscle & skin that blunts my ulna
from its edge i want grit wetted & cold

squint at me with your face hard & mean
you care whether i fly like a flag or like a moth
in the hard deeps between
your mat of creeper & your slow tearing roots

give me stars lost to their shared high chill
in a sky pouring itself mammoth with night

lounge

sly invite you raised to get my audience
yielded to you, rapt & breathing
to the count of four, the corners
where my ribs & hips dig at the mattress.

you knew i'd show, by the back door or any—
you've seen me die down at a whisper
doubled with night & neon, the broken music
in my bones, your fingers rolling out a snare

rhythm, binding, amped to charge tympanum
to tailbone, dive me into arpeggios drawn out & out
over my vertebra riffs—sure & patient, soften
the ivory of my back, fifty-two

stark white keys of bruises healed & scars
gone pale. those grave black half-steps
would clatter, cry, if struck & we'd wail
point blank, shake the windows in their frames

if you walked onstage & took the mike
i'd be as i am now, a rest
between the bars of a rheumatic blues;
i won't be sung. across town,

while your last chords ebb off, i'll wake
breathing with the beat you set me
i'll ache from the wine & write
these words for you: both barren of voice.

fishy parts

slippery spark, you called me, electric eel, even
to the long fins, the touch turned to stun, even to the kelpy
taste. wince & squirm when i'd flood your rooms
with my woman stink (sun on limestone, juniper

berry, sea spray) & leave them shiftier, draped
in chains. you never trusted my eyes, puddle-flat
& round, changing colors like weather.
when you saw my gills pulsing open & closed

in air they couldn't take in, sawn fins struggling
to heave me upright on sand sharp & bright
as milled steel, impotent against the bulk gravity
makes of my belly-pale body—you only tossed

a bucket of cloudy seawater over me. pisces, you said,
you're drowning us both. maybe i was, spilling
over myself, tidal, salt pools bleared in my wake
across your polished floor, the press of my flesh

left soaked into your sheets: you're trekking inland,
taking roads & rivers to wherever they'll meet. never once
did you follow me to the singular rocky coasts
where i split my tail into legs & climb ashore.

becoming a ghost

Groundhog Day/Lupercalia

this is persephone country & i am descending
into her last days as queen, through clouds
drained of both snow & motion, their only art

to chill noon as it passes. early crops, threadbare
as old velvet—who'd believe how the sap in these green smudges
will surge? the week i'm here, yellow crocuses

will announce, the girl's coming back.
queued along sidewalks & wild
in terraces cut to turn hills arable, they'll gleam,

she's coming back. crocuses would know,
wakeful all winter, however addled, however crocked.
the year my mother tried to learn to cuss,
i planted white ones above a cutbank. that spring
when i went to pick them the earth gave out

& dropped me into a storm of black mud & black water
so i had to hand over hand up a tangle of root
discovered by the collapse. inside, tap water burned
rinsing away blood where my fingernails broke off.

every year, to rise into sunlight this cold
& be a daughter again. spring hanging
on her woozy footsteps, her blink at buds
her mother refuses to swell

til she sees her girl safe. to confront
late winter, its forests naked black strokes
in a haze of colorless branches, icy rivers
creeping through them, throttled back

to half their depths. feeling her husband's kiss
hot on her palm, his voice rumbling

they'd make it, they always had. the chilly musk
of blooms too fey for this earth haunting
her hair; then demeter biting her lip

& crying a little, reedy arms enfolding
her daughter's shoulders as she sighs,
now we can get to work. a wonder

the girl never said, come to my place this year,
mother. i'd love to have you underground.

we touch down & cottony remnants
of last summer's flowers shudder, stiff
on their stems. the creek's dammed

to make a cattle pond; our road's dug up
to be paved. persephone tramped through

her own garden, crushed leaves thick as oiltan, petals
like beetles' wings, hauled vines from their roots & dragged them
trailing from her wake-robin's ankles while her mother
flailed at a flurry of clinging, obedient shades.

when she got to the tree, tore the rind
with her teeth, put seed to lip, one, two, how many
before demeter knocked it from her jaw—when the juice
flooded her mouth, tart & impossibly ripe,

how could she ever have stopped, wedded
to that place below, to think she'd have to come back?

l'esprit de l'escalier

for Jeroen

You seem a cathedral, celebrant of the spring
—William Carlos Williams

go on: kick out the chair, dangle & shudder like a minnow, listen
to the static that fills your ears. (had i
wised up.) you blond cipher, aesthete, bleached
remnant of flame. your wary eyes, your twist of a smile

like a twist of paper, the singular twist
of water over gravel as you aggressively await

revolution. you who lived to stare
at excellent throats. savaged; hermetic;
fiercely fallen, precious ash: i was already writing
a dead man. i had woken up afraid

birds were nesting on the other side
of my roof. i mean the ceiling. i can't believe. o witches,

absolve us.

in my dreams *gloria* is an unimpressable redhead in a white coat;
you kiss my forehead high at noon. never a nowhere

minus the no, that unguarded space
we could crib into & never require. a child
might lose itself in the stillness

until ripped away: and down we went. our shadows lay
sharp, hot over grass; you persist

after girl philosophers. today in the library. suddenly shaking
lightly, too old to be speaking in tongues. you obscurantist—the solution
only spoils the problem; i expected

to look at the sun & see a notch
cut out. be born, forced

into freezing light, a cathedral
to troubled surfaces. i'll circle. praise
for the aegean's ridiculous geese, devoted, diving, rising, diving,
squalling, tawny feathers, i'll circle. we unannealed. go on. we twinned

by pieces in duchamp's mirror, his dry dry brush. curve
smoothed smoothing. under. conventional flesh.

this has been only to parody analysis.

so as to appear. to be beautiful, to be broken,
to have vanished. so as to posit yourself
a classical arcade, disintegrating; so as to blow outward,
a frieze, winery & sad young men, fragments

of neck, doorpost, heliotrope leaf. i don't know what you are now
but i hope you haunt me. sit at the edge of your slate-colored sea
& when the wind will, be tumbled westward, veil

the interval between my windowpane & nighttime—blur—

shift of escaping breath. merciless
thin fingers. scribble as i sleep. we sunless,
we intransigent, we with rectitude. beautiful,
dead young man, be in me.

(how else to *implore*, that being the word?)

inventor of lucidity, inventor of violence.

aren't we all. crusts of snow, breaking through as one walks; why else
but to tell me how wrong i am. we smarting
marrow, riven. bones. had i bounded, better, that particular
lake; who'll read me back to myself? crazie glass, brittle, the invincible
invincible. my nihilism is at stake—i hope you know. this
is the basis of decadence. when you turn, like a surface,
or fold—

blur again, dwindle. you anti-ironist, derailed,
you post-poundian. i'm too lonely to be a solipsist: what then
        is harrowed out?

your cheekbones assert
something through a sheen of sweat. (had i. remained

a virgin all her days.) go on—go on—it's time
& past. i'd like to present someone with these sharp edges:
don't let them rub against one another, or lay any part
too far from the rest. (had i bounded.)

it's very obscene but very nice. it's time: in plum blossoms: your body
made of white leaves, your absolution, snowmelt, your pitch brilliance.

with the bare hands

"ain't no latins in the heartland, darlin,"
tendered around a cigarette's trunk
before you tapped ash toward poison ivy leaves

near your hip-waders. like europa
never hung out laundry, never stretched
her summered arms up just to get closer

to the sun's bawdy corus before zeus
hauled her off. or after. like aeneas
never got in a barfight when some *latro*

branded his mother's thighs as laved-over
& not from her spumy birth. "leave the greeks
in greece is all. poems about daddy & jesus

do fine by me." since you did see thomas
wipe his cheek, you heard him blame the sun,
a spur over christ's skinny shoulder,

& the dust its ravin winds roused to stinging brume.
eggplant & old gold, this sky, edged in the dimming east
with clouds, echoing horizon to horizon over blackbirds

picking snails from the clay shore
where, yeah, we got willows, corkscrew & black,
that pale once evening dims in close

around them; we got oak trees whose leaves
spangle creek waters with scraps of rust,
jasper, other minerals that shouldn't float—

once winter shrugs out of the valleys,
which can indeed occur at lupercal & does
if the grain mother eases up early.

like nobody packed their metamorphoses
west, or named their sons cletus or virgil
for the swing in those peakish wails. your eyes pale

& broken like bits of bottle glass, &, "sure
you're from around here, doll?" laughing
how foxes bark; stubbing out the cigarette.

i burrowed my bare toes into wet ground
shot through with roots, leaned back
til the half-bared skin over my spine met

crumbling bark on a cedar we could call, yes, worthy
of lebanon, inhaled to admit its dark perfume
to my blood. some great-great-great of mine,

visigoth, knew: empire belongs to whose tracks
muddy the streets. i nodded. sure. as a heron tossed
up a sunfish & swallowed the lump of it down.

sailors, take warning

the world's only color was red:
rocket red, hot magenta, sun through red
rose petal, cerise or signal flare, borealis,

a hue invented to fuel stars' birth: girl's hair. her eyelids
full but lashless, welded shut
& they did not tremble. she'd wanted a red

that would glow in the dark, deck her
to pirate bullion & spices, stock a brigantine's holds
to the creaky rafters; to catch flowers

tossed by the bevy. the hairdresser
had blinked; she could tell. but money
from her hand & she counted her change

flinchless, then her cane sketched
passage to the street—threatened to lose keel
at the curb but hove to crest right, smoothing

her coronal pageboy. velvet tailcoat in sable,
trousers trimmed to match & satin shirt
charged with dragons. how much brighter,

had that rigging a hardier day to bound from,
instead of spears for a fence mewed to one side, asphalt
across with holes gummed over, mangy buildings

& clouds above neither gray nor white nor silver
but merely covering. the time of year when sunlight
turns to stone & then water, clear like her roaming.

if she go by a wind, say aloof, or keep your loof,
or fall not off; wear no more, keep her to, touch the wind, have a care
of the lee-latch, care smartly. looking to freeboot

the very air, she made herself a blade, clove the day
through its wretched blanch. bend up,
she would. jig her own timbers alist.

at hyacinth's perihelion

she can still see day make room for night.
light that swells & mantles
over the sky's hem. jagged pines

stretch up, black into glow, pulling the sun down
to other haunts. edge of a farm pond with winter

breaking away, mud shore bootheeled, hooved
& frozen into runtish crags. over other hills
people chatter, filling baskets. it's grape country,

michelangelo country, where sunset glazes
limestone blocks. an arch. fallen flat
to the ground, water held by moss imperceptibly crept
into the cracks & joints between stones. while shadows

rise to collude in low spots. land pitches
into an oxbow, one bank shale & sandstone in layers,
the other marshy, full between

of montana inverted. the sun a slice
of flame. bathtub of icy, metallic rain
on the top remaining floor of a blasted hotel; fog below

& horns muttering. the surface is still enough
to count stars in it when they come out.

when the woman approaches, ash, pebbles, broken
bits of tile grate at her bare feet. sand in the crease
behind her toes. she breaks the reflected scene,

& when she opens her jaw what rushes in is thick
& potent as mashed strawberries, what escapes

echoes through the violet evening. the heat in her body stretches
like it has its own limbs, attenuated
at the water's boundary & she wreathes

an antlered, brown vine around her wrist.
she'll sleep curled around mossy rocks. she'll grow gills.

"it wasn't the first time
she'd sealed up a gas tank with maple syrup"

rowdy

made my first dollar pulling a calf
one squally predawn, the waxy caul over its face
white as the frost tatted around the seam
of each hickory nut that swung overhead, storm

heaving in & us some miles from the shed.
made my next dodging a tower of china
that tried to fall on me. pouring coffee

for wags no funnier than the three-year-olds
sick on wine from gallon bottles who'd pitch back
into trays of seamy glassware & ruin, the bride said,
the entire reception. napkins in fan folds

or christmas trees or boxes
like chinese kites; once i showed them to my mother
she made every drawer into a puzzle board. drought years,
we had, & i ended up fishing a dead kitten

out of the cattle tank. old ladies whose skin
was powdery-cool even without talcum

paid me to bring lipsticks in pinks
named for botanicals the earth never grew:
ruby carnation, honey rose, cranberry ice; their eyeshadows
all some blue or some other mauve, asphyxia

muted to match the curtains, & they'd buy
every hand cream i pushed, if i left samples.

this til i pushed up a truck bumper four inches & learned
to putty & sand & shape with a flimsy body file, terra cotta dust
a coat of dry on my tongue, inside my cheeks, darker

where i sweated to a color i could have sold
as hibiscus nude, if i'd made it back to town.
when i did head out, & out, i boarded & bedded
as far as i could on silver glint & bangles of ivory,

the river's bank dark smudges i followed
down the country's middle, my maiden cowboy names:
nancy spurs, muriel the glove, tornado cora. i wore them

in & out of season like suede boots, like hoopskirts
with matching hats. played a saloon a few weeks running
one winter, set up on a stage made of empty tables
& hollered torch hymns over a half-tuned piano.
they called me bethanie jane. never missed a nickel.

came that i served three turns in a drizzle & grim circus,
the ringmaster's satin hat natty with snags, the elephants
chuffing & stubborn, the lady at her bright wheel

tight around the mouth. she said she'd change me
into a grain of corn & let me be ground
down to flour. i shuffled. dealt. tied back
my ashes of gold hair to let the inside light
kindle the lines where fate writes
her cramped hand across ours. billed

as sosostris' second daughter, born
with a veil, imperfectly pale from welsh
witches' blood in my bavarian veins: scrygirl

to women with brittle hair, with crinkles
at their eyes from smiling like divinity,
saccharine & dissolving. to greener girls

whose fathers waited outside, blubbery in overalls
& nothing else, white hair tufting from under
arms gone fallow after years of farming
halfheartedly. to the odd man come to my cabin
just for cards. too long at the edge
of one town & i had to shut the door:

i do not heal comas. voice chipped from flint. hospital's
across the way. lighting candles
anyway; sparks vanishing into rings
in a pot of tea. three turns til i snapped
an axle in a town where even the dead get housed
in dressed stone, & under our feet

nothing but miles down of neither water nor mud
& so both. headed maybe for the yucatán, or on down
to the incan roads where you can run, & run, & stop

only when your breath flags back to you from the peaked air.
but first i've got to pidgin my way
into one of these shotguns, got to get a floor to wax

so when i lay down to study on maps
i'll pin to the ceiling, it'll leave my skirts
clean. got to set a sundial into the lawn.

maybe i'll try on queens, be an elizabeth,
a catherine, arianrhod or helen. if i grew my hair out
i could pull off a crown the way bonnie

pulled off robberies—tell you this—those parade girls
manage. get me some twill, i can dart out a jacket

easy as easy, toss up a banana stand from that tin
& a box of nails, brew you a tonic
to keep pleurisy at bay for three years

& some to go, or guard against pickpockets, or babies,
or the pain under your ribs that brings you to the levee
four nights out of every seven, breaking bottles
against barge hulls. welcome by some name or other

in half the towns from the lakes up north
to the southern keys, meeting ends

by mating one piece just to another, same as electricity, same
as kissing goodnight; what keeps my boots
soled, or puts me in the occasional velvet stitch, what folds
or asserts its jingle on the palm.

subtropic zone

an a.m. too early to bother with the clock, & waking
to vertical rain, to the plush grind
of truck tires wet on my street. to the diminutive twist
in my womb that announces another baby

i won't be birthing. to the north
these same clouds hush themselves earthward
in snow, but here birds start their chirping
over a rosebush toppled by a balmier storm & leaf backs

shine silver untarnished as quartz sand, pierced
by deft red shoots. snow moon,
birch moon. pale & icy all year, even full, but most so
in december. this winter i'm binding back my hunger

for frost, tinted lights, & air that freezes lungs
deep, cider boiling on the stove
to offer a sharp manner of heat. hands clowning
to wrap the cup & feet soaked, tucked to hips

as snow riddles the lot's black first like static
but then the rumpled bowl of the plains
blunted under, stifled, the color of deadwood
beneath piles of frigid white velvet. small moon,

rabbit moon, snow moon. hickory bark under ice
that cracks in day's lesser freeze, glazes roads darker
so cars skate, crush together brilliantly; ice that flounces
windows with cabbage leaves or layered skirts, plated

to new brass when clouds break. steam, here. banana leaves
tattered & waving. every month as it stays warm
i carry the same vague scent. restless
from red core to each fingertip, but this blood

breaks off. rabbit moon, birch moon, starve moon. rain
pours off the street; sky shedding its body
to sate the earth & then some. snow builds, silence & white
stitched by rusty fences. builds. small moon. snow moon.

when morning comes, mist on the interstate
will burn white, kicked up like hoar & i'll drive
to the riverbank, back, singing low as the road hums
in the brackish place folded between my hips.

xmas eve

don't prod, but i had to prod. colloid pool
set into the sand, its center collapsed. here

was my bare toe. & jolt, & ribs, a clutch, sense of hollow
pressed inward: i folded, shaking
as from long hunger, air drenched so my breath
tripped like down a levee with rocks shifting beneath,

finally to fall to the shore. the only color
a juniper bush, berries oiling the breeze
with gin's savor. strike a doorknob with its green

to break the lock, burn its wood
to draw up ghosts, birth in its shade & the child
won't follow you home. tremor inside, gray
light. frigid from sand's damp that crept up my clothes.

jellyfish grew the world's first eyes; they could see to grab
but not what, see night from noon
from a sky of belchy, slow clouds, see twisting away
from the sudden welt. they fill the gulf

with their nickel-sized hatch, clearer spots
mazing the brine. a bell, a tap, sting from its very skin: they thrust

& are away. if i could reopen my lungs. dew;
needles nod & switch against my cheek; the sea throwing itself
into the air. don't prod. if i could drift
& hang downward. if i could hang down

& just see, if i were so astringent,
if i settled the stomach. if i could close & thrust away.

bees in my walls

after a few days i could hear them
when i showered. i'd let my hair tumble
loose & feel brushy feet stealing down my neck

til i scrubbed my fingers across my scalp.
i slept elsewhere & my episcopal neighbor offered
to pour out a jar of honey on the bricks
by my mailbox. they'd abandon

their pearled brood, he said, all their ten or twelve
thousand wings, shiny browns of bee-back
amass over the spoils, leaving silence behind.

you're a writer, you should write something
while they're here, the bee lady told me, bees
are good for writers. takes a lot of stings
to kill a person or even get you a hospital trip,

unless you're allergic. you allergic?
she said. the stories agree, though she told them
with a bucket of screen on her head.
plato had a bee land on his lips as a baby;

maybe virgil too, maybe the buddha. brigid knit tunes to verse
under apple trees in her isle's chalky hills,
& the bees who sucked that nectar mixed rhyme
into their honey. on the news, they bumbled

into & out of eaves like mine. but not mine.
you can't hardly walk down the street,
a man said, without getting stung. he blamed

the frowsy crepe myrtles that lined his sidewalk
with heavy clouds of pink-purple, blooms styled for the peak
of bee vision. no one's lived in the house for ages,

but no one would knock it down. who'd come
so close? rooms filled with rows of comb
& debris layered two feet deep—melted wax,
spoiled honey, a flood of broken-off legs,

headless antennae, hollow thoraces whose velvet
bristles at insect scale to make footholds
on each fat body; generations of moths
laying eggs & their worms eating

up to where the babies get stored; birds
moving in, water bugs, a world in there
& none of it assailable as human skin,
just the wet warmth of hive & a permanent hum

like what i heard when i turned off the tv. evener
than cellos, longer than late summer winds that wither,
like nothing but the concert of clear wings.

it pulsed through the vacuum's drone
when the bee lady gathered them, assuring
they'd be fine, a commodity even; strafing through her voice

when she came back to tell me, it rots, the honey, the wax,
the dead bees & bee parts. it won't make mead or candles.
bust it out of there—rats, mold, who knows

what its syrupy reek could draw in. we broke
through the drywall, & the cells had begun to sag,
liquid to sweat through the grainy wax.

the poetry combine: a collaborative documentary

The Laura Plantation, St. James Parish

even my scalp aches, peels. my shoulders
slough away in the shower, soft fragments,
red peppered with minuscule new scars, seeds

tossed onto coral sand. i go cold white
where my fingertips press but flush again
in one or two heartbeats at the paunchy surface

where i smooth aloe over weeps & cracks. my blood too close
to the air, i can feel its pulse & wash. can't dampen
the sting, don't own clothes gentle enough.

i want my skin back. no one's built
for hours stood still under that heartless southern sun
& no shade to be had. i'd stared off at cane fields

taken by achilles' herb yarrow, may apples,
the palmettos triceratops ate, jerusalem cherry
just blooming; i could pick them out all day.

my journal meanwhile bleached to an ill gray violet
in the trimmed grass at my feet. a border traces
my forehead's edge like an afterimage, clammy divide
as though face & hair failed to meet.

i wanted a compass on top of my foot
but came away with a mangled turtle—tortoise's neck
& very nearly one's flippers if i hadn't stopped
the needle man. he had a book. he'd looked it up.
even took bites out of its shell

to show its wattly legs. his knuckles: r o c k   s t a r
sunfaded to jail tat green. he liked to squint.
his girlfriend wore his work all over: four years

of gigantic twin stars, a cartoon anchor
on her sternum, cherries glistening from her hips, frilly koi
swimming around her belly button & waves
for them to swim in. comic book colors;

i came in for war-era browns, blues, lines
of archival character. no wonder he groused at me

in his kid-smoker voice. but everyone had come, cameras
were rolling & i could breathe
to giggle but not to argue farther. our ink man
dipped in & started drilling.

everybody got a right to sing the blues: tabby thomas,
proprietor, piano rattler. let's hear your licks
he smiles all toothy, let's jam. the bulgarian communist
who spends his midnights assembling techno beats

doesn't get it. though he wrinkles his face
mightily trying. the hollins graduate
who spent a year in ireland & palavers about a *ceilidh*
she'll never hold compares tabby's flirty, twining rolls
to a brahms concerto. the air eddies slate blue

between us & photos of the usual greats
in the usual poses, we order second beers, we tap feet
& nod obediently. the *bastarda ecuadoriana*,
raised in metairie, wants to get it
but listens only to magazine pop & that in her car;

she admits this & reads a blissfully furious poem
about her mother's ignorance of birth control.

i want to get it; after all, country is just blues'
long-legged brother grown up without electricity.

we all got the pain, says tabby, that's why i run a bar
instead of running for president. he puts our drinks
on the house, still grinning. god bless the child.

plank cabins, two rooms each. some sided
with corrugated tin, ragged, some with chicken wire
for windows. fireplaces shared by both families
& a swept plank porch. where our overfed guide

rhapsodized about *compair lapin*, the cajun beast
known in parts east as brer rabbit, how he stowed away
in stories to cross the ocean, burrowed in
with local tongues & animals; how he remained

when brothers & sisters & wives got sold
who knew where or to whom. her arms wobbled
in indian cotton shirtsleeves, picot edged,

as she told how the *lapin* wooed the lion's gorgeous daughter
& got himself a garden plot to boot. pearls buried in gold
on a finger of her right hand; skin freckled
on the biloxi beaches. her eyes pop when she talks

like she's shooting a bad horror movie. we make history
of what's left behind—one bare bulb per room
in the unrestored cabins, boarded shut but you can peek in

at wasps' nests & cobwebs, a string of chunky pink beads, dust
& dry-rattling dead leaves, plaid curtains
blown to the floor. these housed families, she tells us,
through the 1970s. with the fields fallowed,
how did they pay rent?

thirteen ways of looking at kudzu

i
in the last early light, a voodoo woman
shakes her skirts out on a porch
outlined by kudzu. she knows the names
of every weed, their tough or succulent leaves.

ii
green, green grows the kudzu
& the rain drips through it,
gray as paint.

iii
tell me which beauty to laud:
kudzu conquering gardens
or its loose wreath quirked around my wrist;
the tendrils uncurling
or just after.

iv
half a nation washed into the gulf.
the kudzu sunned itself from black soil.

v
kudzu crawls over trees,
thick as green caramel, if caramel
could crawl. scooby-doo ghosts,
they lean over roads & booga-boo.

vi
i was comforted
like an abandoned mill wheel
in kudzu's embrace.

vii
toothless brown paper:
midwinter kudzu
unfurled from a flag pole.

viii
o delta babes, wrapt in cotton,
dream of sweet peas or white daisies,
not this kudzu with violence
in its blossoms to frighten
even the parched bees.

ix
flat on a flat table, billwork bears curves
of kudzu writing across a slant of daylight.
the shadows compare only to the shadows of words.

x
anyone can weave a tent
from kudzu's raveled strands.
anyone can map them into an atlas.
they cannot be baked into a pie.

xi
at dusk, a woman involves herself in song
the way kudzu involves itself in the path
between beds of lavender & rue.

xii
each kudzu vine scrawls an idiolect:
insistent crypticism.

xiii
storms breach the cypresses—
kudzu season has returned.

the bursting miracle

... the miracles which I experience hourly are still of a nature
as to frighten every other human being to death.
—D. P. Schreber

her body is stars & darkness. where she feels anything, she burns,
& these are the stars. tremble; shine. astra

tenebraeque. witless heaven stares down
with its million unsteady eyes, oculi, all gods
through the round opening in the top of a dome,
the oculus. eius corpus, absorbed in staring down

with its stars uncomprehending. for god has no need
to understand human beings but deals only with corpses.

so my body burns, so my skeleton
burns out of my body. you can see where the radiation.

blackened, crannied, the star burning out
of my skeleton. i must bear a star out of my womb. i must diffuse,
grow large of fine fine fine ash & light. yield. the first
is hooks which savage, from my lowest back

to my shoulder blades & pull there til sometimes even the bones
tear free, & i see them spin away through the window
& toward the horizon. at these moments god

sometimes realizes she has overstrained
my body & heals me through sleep, but other times
i lay pooled in agony til a lesser star

recovers me from oblivion & reunites
the pieces of my rent body. the most frightening miracles

are directed against my reason, when i am made to see
beneath someone's skin without warning, when my hearing is assailed

by the stars' voices which resemble kitchen pots
or pieces of metal siding making words
as they fall or crash together. her body is vanishing

darkness. remember how nonsense
erupts. now you have. if the tongue
would. if only light would lie
still. if one. if eyes. eius light tenebraeque. represent

your womb if you must cross. insinuate
that one. lie your tongue still. her body tortures me

laying its starlight on my skin where it crawls,
it is like a gray sea creature, a planarian or swarm
of them latching on with their mouths & rippling

as they feed me away. being so drawn, like blood, like a sketch,
so drawn, i can shake my dreams out like laundry. footnotes
fall to the bottom & claritas. in one the sun
is a shadow on the ground with a hole in it. in one stars bomb down,

searing yellow or green or white, raiding
the grass's dew with their fire, crashing through the window
to explode on my rug or bedframe; the sparks thrown off

thunder miniature, pulveric,
pool & burn, holy lava, collect

& glow & fulm again. god so dreams
in me. how nonsense. why i love a skeleton contra

obscuritatem claritas. at my shoulders' points the stars' voices enter
to conduct oneiromancies & so footnotes

drop like embers from the flesh. each birth lessens
one darkness into another, a sootness,
a likedarkness notdark; we will come
to a gone gray, & frigid, motion lessening

into stillness. a star forced from a body will return
shadows & so shapes. at times i enjoy terrific pleasure
up to my neck while the head is in a bad way. corpus. eius est. her body

watches through the holes in the sky; their witnessing
is to give us our fate: i must render
unto caesura what is hers & when my skin, then

my blood, my bones, when the surface
of my uterus has thinned
this star bursts tenebris from my abdomen, parting

the muscles. it roosts. away. i must almost
be smoke. bemiracled from all sides. i sweat
fire, i quake at the detonations & touched
by light i must blister. the tiny hooks
& the large ones, of steel. of bone, of noise.

vespers, flown

What Thou dost — is Delight
—Emily Dickinson

if he bear it in his arms, be it my body.
if he lay it down, be it tucked into the quiet.
let trill ease to murmur. be me flushed,
tinted beneath the skin, jeweled, smudged,

& if i hold his hands let me kiss them,
let me quake with devotions. if i breathe
be it slow, fortunate. be that i shine

despite whole lives of me spent, brought to beg
& not given; given to beg as though to an embrace.
bound, given haven, straining
& satisfied. if it rise in me like birds

that whirl into lace, then herringbone,
then chessboards, bright webs, craze
of lightning to ground; if it is made of light
& the absence of light, as over sky; if it settle airily:

be it the picture of kneeling, press
of palm to cheek, taste of myself citric & fresh
on his cock, licked from his face. the lips
anywhere, back of my head, top of my wrist,

how anywhere they pin, raze,
how i am bared to bliss. the low
voice, its knowing how the motes of me
knurl together; leather that sings. if these sigh out
let them return. a crash of wings.

if skin, be it given. be it claimed & clean
& written on. be it red running
on pale the color of beach. if he split
it open, be the augury hale, be it witting—

if dark, light candles & let the sky turn. let wax
strike kisses to skin. if i pray,
let the cry plait his pulse to mine.

"this way, if they came for the house
they'd have to leave something behind"

carminae arcana

vi. lovers

after i left, you befriended the chief of police
who told you over whiskeys tossed back at old barney's
how my brash, blind *haa-aahs*
had earned me a file three addresses long,
cars full of cops listening beneath my windows

for the barebacked edge between sex
& something less rapturous. but then none showed

for our one real fight—& even that was all words:
the march night grainy with ice
in its wind, muscular, plunging
between my legs. gouty blood freezing there

to arrow feebly at jeans tangled around my ankles
& me screaming *you wanna fuck*

then let's fuck goddammit screaming
let's wake somebody the fuck up
so you can show me off throaty & screaming *give them*
the show let's light this place up

i got dizzy, hot in the face
& where my voice came from, weightless but dense. the sky split
into a frail dawn; tears itched down my cheeks
to pool above my collarbone. denim
puddled in frozen mud, broken-off grass.

v. hierophant

my eyes green in a mirror with darker rings
at each iris' edge, flecked with brown,
gray & gold; behind me, yours

nearly the same. on sober mornings. sixty-odd years
cumulate between us, reckoned down

to one night, my arms around your calves, belly
flat to the floor with what drag i had & could it hold
against the scotch, the rifle's weight, could gravity

help keep safe your ex-wife, the lawyer
in her bed—would we all just fold

& break like dry-rotted boards?
barely, no, but new year's, your eyes beyond
focusing on mine, voice splintered. *before all the gods*

i marry you. gravel shifting under your cowboy boots
as you slouched toward me. *i goddamn marry you*
& me suddenly sober, saying anything to get us back

to the hotel. wet grass somewhere, tree bark
grating the side of my neck. taking a whole cherry pie
to our room. then morning, & would you look
at that, her footprints still greased on the windshield.

home, & winter, & burnt to the bones.

iv. emperor

nothing broken or breaking, but my heart
so full it bulged against my ribcage, forced blood
into my mouth. tight like steel bending

i whispered *son of a bitch* because i'd met
your mother, witnessed her vampish posture,
her glances like light through blue glass, avian hug.
wet smiling cunt. i'd seen pictures of her from age
fourteen, thirteen, lush in her arms & everywhere

& her eyes as old as they were ever going to get.
this was when i showed you my swollen lips,
too raw to cry or even piss, the shade
& texture of an african violet's petals, welted

by what had worn your jeans
white at the zipper. i could itch with sour sweat
from cutting back hedges, ache like my gut was rusting out

while i sat still, didn't matter. you said i got you going
just like a old junkyard dog & i'm supposed
to go *all a-flutter.* that easy. my chest slicked

with your sweat & shed hairs. in the window-light
across the room, my pages fanned out
for your felt tip. you could barely hide
your shoulders strutting out.

iii. empress

dream: gazebo in marsh, air rank with pollen
& the breathings-out of mold, yellow yellow sun
painting my arms & legs. the fact of a small crowd
of less importance than the sand & dew

creeping up my dress, antique white, the fact
of sunlight second to that of breeze, the damp drag
of hem across calf, drag & back as ankles
meet water at its surface & then my hand

into another. yes, i wake heady & warm.
he's a recovering accountant trying his hand
at motorcycle restoration; awake, he wants nothing

with me. i did read his palms. yes. as if i shouldn't wish
to feel young for a change after putting on this cozy paunch
tending you. dream: your arms
around my shoulders, your shoulder still

the wrong height, fingers princessing the seam
of my spine. in your living room, my matter-of-fact
breaking open all over you, your rough coos, the cloy

your voice lays down. the same voice smaller
on the phone: how could i be tapping home
bent tracks to mend my windows,
how could tweed fit my length of limb?

ii. priestess

roses' appley scent, chenin blanc, johnny cash rumbling
at top volume. driving for santa fe after work
so we'd get there in time for sunrise. the always out
always down scalp first of massage; a crisp shirt,
salad, morning; wrapped wrists. all the parts

you never got right, i conjure to travel
the miles now cabled between us to temper your lust
for jealousy. as for me: cat in a cage

doesn't even begin. *find yourself a boyfriend*
as if one can have some fattish, burly individual
lift down a suitable partner from a stack
of treated timber. as if one can't dance alone,

or with friends who stay friends, as if barefoot
says pregnant, tender, & not toes reaching
between roots on the slow climb up a cutbank—

as if climbing were only for vines. dream: an abler ex
writes me on rumpled paper napkins, ballpoint letters
stained by coffee. he underlines so i can't mistake
his translation. headstone trade. shall i explain

the fact of order? the hands & how to stop them
from shaking. shall i cast about? every late call, your words
stumbling, & the trough, the beg from you, now far north.

i. magician

dream: i make you bend me over a bed, starchy
motel sheets meeting my palms & thighs:
i have to hide a massive cock hanging pendant
from my crotch, have to hunch

like i'm ill so you won't see it swing, thick
as your forearm & nearly as long. when i come

it's only tears & when i wake it's wind scudding
through leaves like fingers tangling in a stranger's hair.
takes a long time to get down from what i knew

into what i saw, with the river here curdling
through its land til both run brown as gravy & not
half so smooth. with the cheap vaults two blocks up
where a hundred days in, a body burns to ash

& can be blown clean into a tin urn
or onto the tough southern grass. with the hours
while late turns to early & then over. years later, states away,

it's like old times. tweedling guitars upstairs, sleazy bass
& brass, smoke oozing into my room. the cheap music
of corn whiskey tumbling over ice & my teeth
clenched against the one sure thing:

you pounding away at a novel, *boning the muse,*
baby. rattling your history into being.

on a boy named for war, enrolled
in my afternoon comp class

chest light & empty, legs feeling as though they're still
learning to walk: you must understand i can make no answer
here. you lean low over me like the appled tree but broad-shouldered
like adam. slender spikes of hair, gelled this morning, curl

over your forehead; one hand half-wraps the corner of my desk
& your scent warms the air between us, part bull musk, part hay.
one fingertip rises to your lips, denting their angel curve
as you watch me read—black ink scrawled, but carefully,

into quatrains: all lips & skin, sweat, & how you dream,
& my legs, the one line each from toe to hip. a light like steel
on flint flares in your eyes, momentary, momentary,

& in any other world, i would have you, too. what hours
you must have spent, eyelids atremble, seeing my body "cradled
like a dolphin in her own ocean" in those muscular arms.

red*star

222 Laurel St., Baton Rouge, LA

here's plaster, cracked last time the swamp shifted
beneath this ghost of a downtown. red lights
swing above the bar like thirsty aeronauts

as someone in flared pants bends forward
to read jukebox pages turning
one button-press at a time. a bony right hand

angles a cigarette away from a girl's waist, skirt
slouched down around her hips: leather
on leather as he leans her into him & talks

into her ear. & while the night rises
over us in smoke & juke noise, a sad old bungle slumps
deep into velveteen. if he's lucky

someone will stumble across his knees,
sloppily grinning, sugary glaze in her eyes, unsteady
giggle. maybe that china doll with the ponytail

jeweled to her scalp. she'll spill her sidecar,
maybe not notice how his face sags
like it's hanging from a nail, or how maths glare

from his eyes. she'll follow him like a map.
i'm just waiting for the lights to come up, give
my high heels an excuse to carry me

into cool air & laughter dying off. outside, a sky lit
mostly from below, & when i go to my car, rain
piling roundels on the windshield.

mistress

you lap between my legs & leave me
sodden you lizardly odalisque with eyes
blue as blood without breath so with a low sigh
out tumble figures like shadows the idle page leaving my chest

the feeling of tramped through you're clutching
between your legs some virtuoso of fingers in clay

or moaning bow on strings or pigment or wood chisel ballpoint
pressed against paper your white body their desperate
closures near on victory & baying joined

to shudder up through the net woven
by stars & the stories that link them

don't smile your eyes blue as the west
the night to the west with ice fallen
to clear the air & puffing breath the indigo west bleached
put it off help me scribble out

lignous blood gotta get some room
in my lungs don't you smile at me when i would mute myself
for a life on the far side of the page

cunning you cunt you ken knowledge as in occult
your breasts even as numbers skin like white ash
your hands' lunatic governance i miss
the rigid salt of cock pressed into my tongue
brawny channel bulging & beating the summoning-up
of self & giving over

to the riot at my center giving gone away
god you goddess i'd have been you

if i'd been born to grace cling like damp
pages like ice in winter's fullest sun
can't move as if i were a river silting out
its curl whisper between reeds

whatever color your skin you're dark
as what rains in my dreams fey
no answer & you smile

at me when i roil tight & channeled
swindler ink ophelia lazing in bed

spots on the sheets & all of them black absence black slatternly
gift from my lady of smooth account no channels cut

nights twisting leg against leg praying
a cool to this crave
spots on my sheets all black

you every dank sacred place you temple
the spring & so near the sun you leave
them to wrecked wings on the mountainside i pray

don't smile at me you dead tongue give me one
one ride through & on but you just feed me
more lines you cunt you rotten cunt

descendant

i have come down for a cup of tea. i couldn't sleep.
i have come down to check the cellar door. for a glass of wine

after my bath. to search for an earring i lost
this evening. i have come down to get the cat

out of the cellar. his head is dusty & i call him a brat
before we go to bed. i wanted a cup of tea

but the stove has gone out so instead i will have
a saucer of milk. i am not art; i am a woman. i want to drink

tea sitting in the window seat, velvet
curtain folded around me, frosty black glass

to my right. i will make art
of my skin's dampness. you bare me

to this ochre night; i can smell your turpentine, i can hear your spatula
slopping in the paint like it's a lakeshore

where you've dropped your field glasses.
i am an ochre woman. a woman of old brass.

halfway down i raise my arm
to push back dripping hair, to scratch my head

as i squint down the stairs. my body gives back
the bare dark & the thin light from this candle. see also the flame

dangerously close to my nipple. i thought i was alone; i am a glass
    of woman
& you have shattered me from cellar to ceilings. see also the arc

as calf muscle swings the body from step to step. i have come down
for the large mirror in the dining room,

i want to see myself in one piece. i love the gilt
wrought over its frame, how buttery

even a thin layer of gold feels. i love a good glass of wine
after a bath. as i step down, night

breezes between my knees, under my arms. see how tiny is the light
on my fingernails. i want to play you at chess. i want to stand with you

before a mirror as big as a bed
& watch you shiver. see also the marble floor, black

& glossy. i am not art, i am a glass of chardonnay. roll me
in your mouth. i want to butter your tongue.

the space from polestar to dog star

it's pushing a boat out onto a lake,
then sitting on the dock to watch it float
away. it's the water's surface, disturbed

then subsiding, & woody green
everywhere you can see into it. the dock pilings
soaking your jeans; the slick scum
so when you stand up, you have to walk

like an indian guide. it's pitching pennies
into a mall fountain. by small handfuls.
not the shiny ones, the old ones. the ones so tarnished

their odor prickles in your nostrils,
into the corners of your eyes; they wouldn't ring
if you tossed them onto pavement

& so into the water. it's heat shimmer. rippling
in front of a plywood flat slung across sawhorses

at an auction, its surface packed over
every inch with carnival glass: turquoise,
sunset orange, purple. blackberry purple.
eggplant skin, what they call aubergine
in the catalogs. it's the sheen

plated over each pressed curve
of tulip, cabbage, acanthus, every facet
of kite-shaped diamond. it's in the milk glass,

the dozens of hens on dozens of nests
from all the rooms in the farmhouse brooded
together. in how the rainbows half-shift. as you walk

around the bowed table. the grass rucked up
in clumps around its legs. it's only just
the baby blues, it'll pass. it's taking out basting thread
& how you snap it, leave red wisps in the chambray

because they'll come out in the wash. it's sliding
a sheaf of pages into a mailbox, the moment of grate

ringing in the skin just under your nails
as you shut the lid. it's a glint. in the bare spot

where the paint has rubbed away. it's coffee
in a paper cup. the sugar. in packets. it's the last time
you vacuum rooms in a house you're about to move out of.

medea

for R.

she had to know he'd never
come home. when he kissed her
as though that day she had turned
unholy. did she set to her loom

anyway. did she. think how she had run
to him. dew falling to her skin & cool,
every door silent, the obedient
iron. lips set beneath henna,

cask of poisons at his call. did she
miss the sweet eastern oil already,
scenting the air where she'd served
hecate, did she ache in her belly

to run ritual. her hands pungent,
sticky, with rosemary & myrrh.
in her husband's sleeping breath
did she hear her sandals' hush echoing

through the dark halls. did she feel
the serpent's head heavy & the shape
of a folded packet of seed, resting
in her lap while she traced histories

out of his scales. her dragons
had mutinied, hauled their chariot
back to helios' isle, scared his cattle
into the ocean. but would she ever

need them again. her body chapped
now by the greek sun. if going, ungently,
& what that means. did she remember,
did she. lost her only brother

for jason's sake. & did she even blink
at the blame. when she parted
her sons' brown skins with the knife,
did she see the wake behind

like one man swimming a river. the case's
catch mangled in the years between. venom
hot in her throat. throat like linen
twisted across stones, stiff with salt

after the tide. did she say,
we've spurned the gods, so even brilliance
like this day collapses on us. did she say, apology
is ours. did she. did she. did tears

spill off her face & did she see
the spreading edge of blood where they hit,
bite back her breath to see the red
curl in anyway, more wet

only an excuse to run farther.
& when the women called her
to come out front, could she speak
at all, or did she. just stare

at the tousled curves
of an ivy bed. the hard edges
of light laying in rainwater,
sharper than the torch kindled above.

about the author

A former artist's model, astrophysics major, Avon lady, and professional fortuneteller, Victoria Brockmeier has published poetry in *LIT*, *New Letters*, *Pleiades*, *Spoon River Poetry Review*, *Boston Review*, and other journals. She earned her MFA at Louisiana State University and is currently writing her dissertation, titled "Apostate, Sing This World Forth: Avant-Mythopoetic Encounters With Doubt, Chaos, and Secular Community" at the University at Buffalo, where she also coordinates dove|tail, a series of poetry readings and chapbooks.